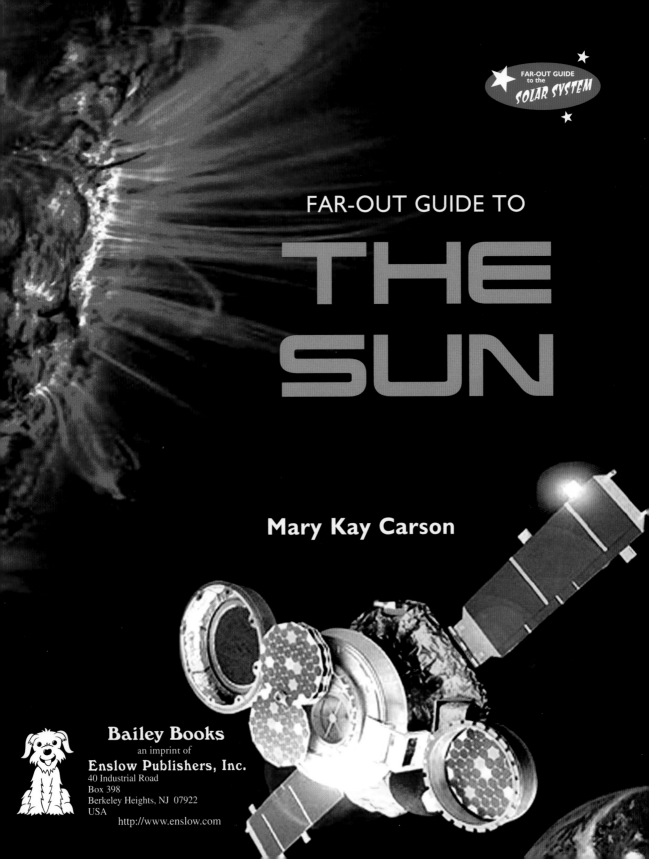

FAR-OUT GUIDE to the **SOLAR SYSTEM**

FAR-OUT GUIDE TO

THE SUN

Mary Kay Carson

Bailey Books
an imprint of
Enslow Publishers, Inc.
40 Industrial Road
Box 398
Berkeley Heights, NJ 07922
USA
http://www.enslow.com

For Abigail Mae Fry, a star as bright as the Sun.

Bailey Books, an imprint of Enslow Publishers, Inc.

Copyright © 2010 by Mary Kay Carson.

Library of Congress Cataloging-in-Publication Data

Carson, Mary Kay.
    Far-out guide to the sun / Mary Kay Carson.
        p. cm. — (Far-out guide to the solar system)
    Includes bibliographical references and index.
    Summary: "Presents information about the sun, including fast facts, history, and technology used to study
it"—Provided by publisher.
    ISBN 978-0-7660-3179-1 (Library Ed.)
    ISBN 978-1-59845-180-1 (Paperback Ed.)
    1. Sun—Juvenile literature. 2. Solar system—Juvenile literature. I. Title.
QB521.5.C376 2011
523.7—dc22
                            2008050039

Printed in China

052010 Leo Paper Group, Heshan City, Guangdong, China

10 9 8 7 6 5 4 3 2 1

To Our Readers: We have done our best to make sure all Internet addresses in this book were active and appropriate when we went to press. However, the author and the publisher have no control over and assume no liability for the material available on those Internet sites or on other Web sites they may link to. Any comments or suggestions can be sent by e-mail to comments@enslow.com or to the address on the back cover.

Image Credits: Centre National d'Etudes Spatiales, p. 38; Headquarters – Great Images in NASA (NASA-HQ-GRIN), p. 39; Japan Aerospace Exploration Agency (JAXA), pp. 12–13; NASA, pp. 3, 29, 40, 43; NASA Johnson Space Center, pp. 32, 37; NASA, ESA, and K. Noll (STScI), p. 7; NASA/Goddard Space Flight Center Scientific Visualization Studio, p. 15; NASA/JPL-Caltech, pp. 1, 31, 35, 36; NASA/JPL-Caltech/NRL/GSFC, p. 24; NASA/JPL-Caltech/S. Stolovy (SSC/Caltech), p. 6; Shutterstock, pp. 4–5, 8; SOHO (ESA & NASA), pp. 10, 14, 16, 18, 20; Tom Uhlman/www.tomuphoto.com, p. 42; U.S. Air Force photo by Senior Airman Joshua Strang, p. 22.

Cover Image: NASA/JPL-Caltech

CONTENTS

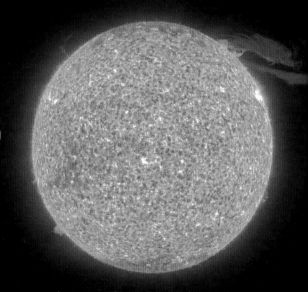

INTRODUCTION

Sun

THE Sun makes up 99.8 percent of the total mass of our solar system. More than one million Earths could fit inside the Sun.

When you look at stars in the night sky, you are actually seeing thousands of suns. A sun is the star in the center of a solar system. Like all stars, our solar system's sun is a ball of glowing gas. Our sun—we call it "the Sun"—even has a star name. Its name is Sol. Sol is a yellow star of medium size. It seems big to us because it is so much closer than other stars. But our sun is a pretty ordinary star. There are billions of others like it in the universe. You will learn lots more far-out facts about the Sun in this book. Just keep reading!

LIFE OF SOL

The Sun bathes our planet in light. Plants use the Sun's energy to make food. Sunlight's heating of Earth creates wind. The Sun's rays evaporate water into clouds that make rain. Without the Sun, life could not exist on Earth. In fact, without the Sun, there would be no solar system at all. The planets, moons, comets, and asteroids all formed from the leftovers of Sol's birth.

THIS illustration shows a swirling cloud of gas and dust surrounding a newly born star. Planets, moons, asteroids, and other solar system stuff will eventually form when chunks of leftovers clump together.

More than 99 percent of the mass in our entire solar system is the Sun.

The Sun seems unchanging to us. It rises each day and sets each night. But all stars are born, live, and eventually die. Our sun has a long life, thankfully. It formed out of a cloud of dust and gas about 5 billion years ago. It will shine like it does now for another 5 billion years or so, and then slowly begin to die.

Yet the Sun changes from year to year as it spins and speeds through space. Sometimes it is calm. But other times it rages and boils with solar flares and storms that can hurl danger toward Earth. What causes these storms? How dangerous are they to us? Scientists have found out a lot about the Sun. But they still have much to learn about the star of our solar system.

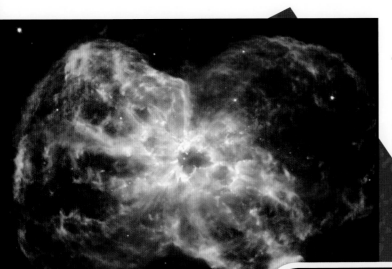

THIS *Hubble Space Telescope* image shows a star much like our own Sun at the end of its life. It has shed its outer layer of gas.

FAR-OUT FACT

HOW WILL THE SUN DIE?

Nothing lasts forever, not even the Sun. In about 5 billion years, the Sun will start to grow old. It will swell up and get hotter for a while, swallowing up Mercury and cooking Earth. Toward the end of its life, the Sun will blow off its outer layers. Its center will shrink into a dense ball. From then on Sol will grow cooler and its light fainter and fainter as it runs out of fuel.

CHAPTER I

WATCHING SPACE WEATHER

At 2:45 A.M. on March 13, 1989, a powerful storm knocked out power in Quebec, Canada. Six million people lost electricity. Some were stuck in elevators or dark offices. Many woke up in freezing-cold homes without heat. Others had to drive on roads without traffic lights. The subway and airport shut down. Schools and businesses closed. It took nine hours to get the lights back on and cost the power company 10 million dollars.

What kind of storm caused such a big blackout? Not a blizzard, tornado, or any other kind of earthly weather. The blackout was triggered by a storm on the Sun—so-called space weather. "It can be difficult for people to believe that space weather can affect life on Earth," said scientist Larry Combs. Combs is a space weather forecaster. "But in fact it can have a tremendous impact on communication and navigation systems, satellites, electric power grids, and astronauts working and living in space."

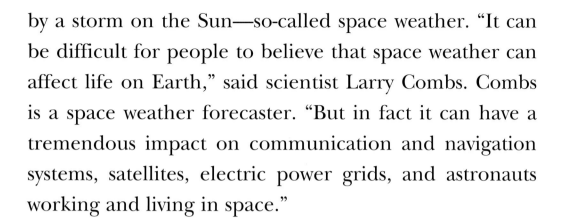

FAR-OUT FACT

EARTH'S SUN-POWERED SEASONS

Earth spins on a tilt, which creates our seasons. The part of the Earth that is having summer is tilted toward the Sun. It gets more than twelve hours of sunlight per day. Summer sunlight is also stronger. The summer Sun is higher in the sky, like a lamp directly overhead. The part of Earth that is having winter is tilted away from the Sun. Wintry parts of Earth have fewer than twelve hours of sunlight a day. Winter sunlight is weaker because the Sun is lower in the sky. It comes in at an angle, which spreads out the light.

Chromosphere

Convective Zone

Radiative Zone

Core

Photosphere

Corona

THE core is where the Sun makes its energy. All the pressure and heat in the core smashes the Sun's hydrogen fuel, changing it into helium. This releases energy that slowly travels outward through the radiative zone. In the convective zone, rising and falling hot gases carry heat to the Sun's surface, or photosphere. Just above the surface is the chromosphere, where solar flares happen. The corona is the Sun's outer atmosphere. It is a halo of hot gas, hotter than the Sun's surface.

STORMY SUN SEASONS

A storm is a violent burst of activity. Tornadoes are bursts of wind. Blizzards are bursts of snow. Solar storms are bursts of activity on the Sun. How the Sun's activity affects Earth is called space weather. Solar storms can shoot clouds of invisible particles toward Earth. These can mess up electric and telephone lines, block out radio signals, and damage orbiting satellites. Stormy space weather can interfere with and damage some of the modern technology we depend on.

Solar storms are just part of living with an ever-changing star. The Sun is not a simple ball of gas hanging in space. It has an atmosphere, a surface, middle layers, and a center core. Within the Sun, hot dense gases somersault. This constant churning makes electric currents that create a magnetic field. The Sun is a huge, powerful spinning magnet!

The Sun also has eleven-year seasons, called solar cycles or sunspot cycles. A sunspot is a dark patch on the Sun's surface. Sunspots are areas where the Sun's magnetic field is concentrated. When there are more

HINODE is a Japanese satellite with three solar telescopes on board. The spacecraft was launched in 2006. It studies solar wind and the Sun's magnetic field.

sunspots, there is more unstable magnetic energy. More unstable magnetic energy creates more solar storms. The solar maximum is the part of the solar cycle when the most sunspots appear. And it is also when the most solar storms happen. Sunspot groups often cause severe solar storms, so scientists track them carefully.

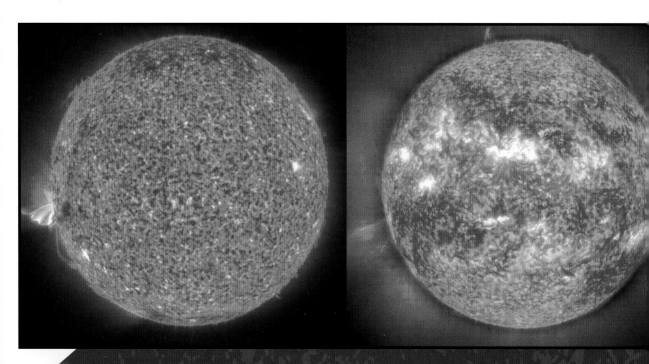

THESE *Solar and Heliospheric Observatory (SOHO)* images compare the Sun's activity at solar maximum (right), when there are more solar storms, and calmer solar minimum (left). *SOHO* is a robotic spacecraft that moves around the Sun with Earth.

A solar flare came from the sunspot shown here in late 2006. *Hinode* took the close-up photograph.

FORECASTING THE SUN

Tracking sunspots and predicting solar storms is what a space weather forecaster does. Special telescopes constantly take pictures of the Sun and measure the energy it creates. Satellites and space probes, such as *SOHO* and *Hinode,* also study the Sun. They send their images and

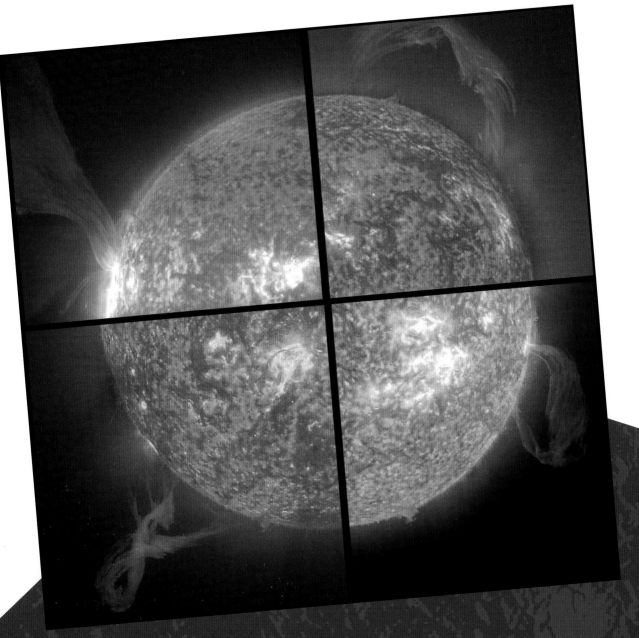

THIS is a *SOHO* collage of four solar prominences blasting from the Sun's chromosphere. The hottest areas are white, and darker red areas are less hot.

measurements back to scientists on Earth. Computers help sort all the information so space weather forecasters can see patterns and predict what is on the way.

Space weather forecaster Larry Combs explained how he does it. The scientist pointed to an image of the Sun on a computer screen. "We look at sunspots," he said, pointing to a dark patch on the Sun about the size of fourteen Earths. "We also look at prominences," Combs said, pointing to a giant bright arch of gas leaping off the Sun's surface. "Both of these areas can create solar storms." Either can explode in an instant, sending out a blinding flash of energy called a solar flare. Solar flares can reach temperatures of 45 million degrees Celsius (80 million degrees Fahrenheit)—nearly three times as hot as the Sun's core. Some solar flares stretch thousands of kilometers into the Sun's atmosphere, or corona. Each solar flare hurls huge amounts of charged particles and magnetic energy into space. The Quebec blackout on March 13, 1989, was caused by solar flares three days earlier. They spewed a cloud of charged particles into space traveling millions of kilometers per hour toward Earth. "The storms were an eye-opening event for

THE bright spot on the right is the most powerful solar flare ever recorded. *SOHO* took this image in 2003. The added green color helps make the flare stand out.

FAR-OUT FACT

BRAVING A SOLAR STORM IN SPACE

The Sun was at solar maximum in October 2003. A giant solar flare shot out toward Earth from a sunspot the size of Jupiter. The solar storm threatened astronauts aboard the International Space Station. Out in space, the charged particles and solar rays carried by solar storms can be very dangerous to humans. Thankfully, astronauts had enough warning time. They canceled all spacewalks and safely tucked themselves deep inside the space station's protective core.

understanding what can happen when the Sun has its violent moments," remembered Combs.

SOUNDING THE ALARM

Space weather forecasters are also on the lookout for coronal mass ejections (CMEs). CMEs are explosions in the Sun's atmosphere, or corona. Space weather scientists call them the hurricanes of space weather because they are so huge and powerful. One CME can send 20 billion tons of dangerously charged material into space in a giant cloud. "We see CMEs all the time from the Sun," said Combs. But a CME is only dangerous when it is facing Earth. Charged particles shooting off a CME on the Sun's backside head away from Earth. Scientists become concerned when a CME-making area on the Sun directly faces Earth. They call it the kill zone. "It's where all the energies are coming straight toward Earth," said Combs.

The Earth is not defenseless. Its own magnetic field protects it from much of what the Sun sends out. Earth's spin and sloshing liquid metal center create a magnetic field that wraps around our planet like a shield. Earth's magnetic field pushes away the normal stream of charged particles from the Sun, just as one magnet repels another. This normal stream is called the solar wind, and it causes few problems. But when a solar storm hits, Earth's protective shield can be overpowered. Charged particles and magnetic energy that reach through Earth's

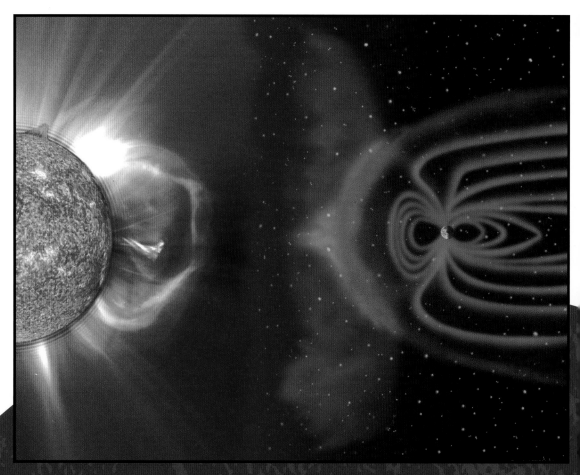

THIS illustration shows a coronal mass ejection (CME) blasting off the Sun and a solar storm of charged particles hitting Earth's magnetic field (the blue lines).

SOLAR SUPER STORM

In September 1859, six months before the American Civil War began, a huge solar storm hit Earth. Sunspots spat out several solar flares, and on September 1st, the Sun blasted out a huge coronal mass ejection (CME) directly at Earth. Back in 1859 there were no power lines, telephones, radios, or satellites to harm. But telegraph wires on poles crisscrossed the United States and Europe. These wires exploded, starting fires in many places. Scientists believe that a solar storm of this strength would cause all kinds of problems with today's modern technology.

protective shield can overload power lines and disturb radio signals.

Thankfully, space weather forecasters are there to sound the alarm. "Our primary job is to monitor the Sun and to put out the alerts, watches, and warnings for solar activity," said Combs. Having time to prepare for solar storms makes a big difference. There is a lot engineers can do to prevent damage to power and telephone lines—if they know what is coming. Controllers can

THIS aurora blazes over Alaska.

THIS aurora blazes over Alaska.

FAR-OUT FACT

AURORAS

Auroras are colorful, moving curtains of light in the sky caused by the solar wind hitting the atmosphere. Auroras usually appear near the North and South Poles, where Earth's magnetic field bends toward Earth's surface. But during solar storms, Earth's protective shield can be overpowered. This allows solar wind to enter far from the poles, and auroras may appear nearer the equator. During the 1859 super solar storm, auroras were seen as far from the poles as Rome, Cuba, and Hawaii.

temporarily shut down satellites to protect them, and communication radios can switch channels. Everyone knows how important storm warnings are. "When we have a tornado warning we know the urgency to get that out to the public to let people know what's happening," said Combs. "It's the same thing with space weather."

SUN AT A GLANCE

Diameter: 1,391,000 kilometers (864,400 miles)

Volume: 1,300,000 Earths

Mass: 332,900 Earths or 1,989,000,000,000,000,000 trillion kilograms

Gravity: A 75-pound kid would weigh 2,100 pounds

Position: Center of our solar system

Day Length (one spin): 609 hours, seven minutes

Year Length (one orbit around galaxy): 225 million Earth years

Color: Yellow

Star Type: Yellow dwarf

Age: 4.6 billion years

Composition (by mass): 70 percent hydrogen; 28 percent helium; 2 percent other elements, including oxygen, carbon, neon, nitrogen, magnesium, iron, and silicon

Surface Temperature: 5,500 degrees Celsius (10,000 degrees Fahrenheit)

Namesake: Sol is the Roman sun god.

Symbol:

★ The Sun is a glowing ball of mostly hydrogen and helium gases.

★ The Sun is a kind of medium-sized yellow star called a yellow dwarf. There are millions of yellow dwarf stars in the Milky Way galaxy.

★ The Sun is about halfway through its life span. In about 5 billion years, it will begin to die.

★ The Sun will get hotter before it dies.

★ Sol is twice as big as most stars in the Milky Way galaxy.

★ Almost the entire mass of the solar system—99.86 percent—is the Sun. All the planets, moons, asteroids, and comets make up the other 0.14 percent.

★ More than one million Earths could fit inside the Sun.

★ Sunlight makes life on Earth possible. It provides the energy for photosynthesis and warms our planet. The Sun drives our planet's weather, creates seasons, and stirs the ocean currents.

★ Earth's seasons are created by its tilt, which leans the summer areas toward the Sun and the winter areas away from the Sun.

★ The Sun's light energy is what travels through space. Sunlight becomes heat when it hits Earth's atmosphere and surface.

★ A solar eclipse happens when the Moon gets between the Sun and the Earth, blocking our view of the Sun and casting a shadow on Earth.

Layers of the Sun Fast Facts

★ Scientists divide the Sun into six regions, or layers: the core, the radiative zone, the convective zone, the photosphere, the chromosphere, and the corona.

★ The core is the center of the Sun. It is the hottest layer, 15 million degrees Celsius (27 million degrees Fahrenheit).

★ The core is where the Sun's light and heat energy is created.

★ The Sun's hydrogen fuel releases huge amounts of energy when it is changed into helium.

★ In one second, the Sun makes 386 billion billion megawatts of energy—more than all the energy humans have used in all of civilization.

★ Energy from the core moves to the radiative zone, where it bounces around like a pinball.

★ In the convective zone, temperatures cool to below 2 million degrees Celsius (3.5 million degrees Fahrenheit).

★ Heated gas in the convective zone churns and moves up to the photosphere, where temperatures drop to about 5,500 degrees Celsius (10,000 degrees Fahrenheit).

★ The photosphere is a 500-kilometer-thick (300-mile-thick) layer of the Sun. It is often called the Sun's surface, though it is not solid.

★ The Sun's light radiates from the photosphere, taking eight minutes to reach Earth.

★ Above the Sun's surface is the chromosphere and then the outer atmosphere, called the corona.

★ The corona is made of very thin gases. Its temperature can be as high as 2 million degrees Celsius (3.5 million degrees Fahrenheit), hundreds of times hotter than the Sun's surface.

Solar Wind and Storms Fast Facts

★ The solar wind is a stream of charged particles constantly released by the Sun.

★ The Northern and Southern Lights, or auroras, are created by the solar wind hitting Earth's atmosphere at the poles.

★ Solar storms are bursts of magnetic activity on the Sun that can shoot charged particles toward Earth.

★ Solar storms can blast out as much mass as Mount Everest contains.

★ Solar storms can interfere with or damage technology, including electric and telephone lines, cell phones, and satellites.

★ Radiation released during some solar storms can also endanger astronauts working in space.

★ Most solar storms come from sunspots, concentrated areas of magnetic field on the Sun's surface.

★ The Sun has an eleven-year season called a solar cycle or sunspot cycle.

★ Solar storms are more common during solar maximum, the part of the Sun's eleven-year cycle when more sunspots occur.

Sun Timeline
of Exploration and Discovery

Circa 384 B.C.—Aristotle observes the Sun by projecting an image of it on the ground through a hole poked in a screen.

325 B.C.—Theophrastus is first to identify sunspots.

150 A.D.—Ptolemy wrongly writes that the Sun and planets orbit Earth.

1543—Copernicus suggests that the Sun, not Earth, is the center of the cosmos.

1610—Galileo studies sunspots by projecting an image of the Sun through his telescope.

1645–1715—The Maunder Minimum, a time of unusually low sunspot activity, occurs and may cause the Little Ice Age on Earth.

1840s—Heinrich Schwabe discovers that sunspots have an eleven-year cycle.

1845—The Sun is photographed for the first time.

1859—Richard Carrington discovers solar flares. Huge solar storm hits Earth, destroying telegraph wires and creating auroras as far south as the tropics.

1860—Observers of a total solar eclipse see the first recorded coronal mass ejection.

1908—George Ellery Hale shows that sunspots contain powerful magnetic fields.

1950s—Rockets sent above Earth's atmosphere measure invisible X-rays and ultraviolet rays from the Sun.

1958—*Pioneer 1* space probe discovers the solar wind.

1973–1974—Space station *Skylab* observes the Sun with solar telescopes.

1975–1976—Space probes *Helios 1* and *Helios 2* come within 43 million kilometers (26 million miles) of the Sun.

1984—National Solar Observatory is set up, including solar telescopes in New Mexico and Arizona that track and observe the changing Sun and space weather.

1989—A solar storm causes blackouts in North America.

1991–2001—Satellite *Yohkoh* studies solar rays.

1994–2008—Space probe *Ulysses* studies polar regions of the Sun.

1995—*Solar and Heliospheric Observatory (SOHO)* space probe begins studying the Sun's interior, atmosphere, and wind.

2004—Sample-return probe *Genesis* crashes to Earth after spending three years collecting solar wind particles.

2006—*Hinode* satellite begins studying solar wind and the Sun's magnetic field.

2010—*Solar Dynamics Observatory* satellite to begin studying solar activity, space weather, and their impacts on Earth.

2015—Spacecraft *Solar Probe+* to launch and enter the Sun's corona.

CHAPTER 2

CAPTURING A PIECE OF THE SUN

Genesis is a mission to find out what exactly makes up the Sun. While the Sun is mostly hydrogen, it also contains small amounts of other atoms—like oxygen, carbon, iron, and nitrogen. Scientists want to know the particular mix of the Sun's atoms. Why? Because the mix of atoms in the Sun is the same as the cloud of gas and dust that started our solar system 4.6 billion years ago. "It's an exciting opportunity to view back in time to the very beginning to the birth of our solar system and try to understand where we came from," explained Eileen Stansbery, a scientist on the *Genesis* project.

Genesis is a robotic spacecraft that collected some bits of Sun—solar wind particles—for scientists to study. It was launched in 2001. *Genesis* traveled one million miles away to escape Earth's protective magnetic shield. Then it opened its collectors to the solar wind. The collectors are thin, round wafers. They are made of strong, pure materials—gold, sapphire, silicon, and aluminum.

THIS illustration of *Genesis* shows how the solar collectors opened, sunbathing the wafers in invisible solar wind.

31

When fast-moving solar wind particles slam into the wafers, they become trapped, like marbles sunk into mud.

Solar wind particles "are so tiny that you can't even see them," explained Stansbery. "But we collected billions and billions . . . to analyze." *Genesis* collected bits of the

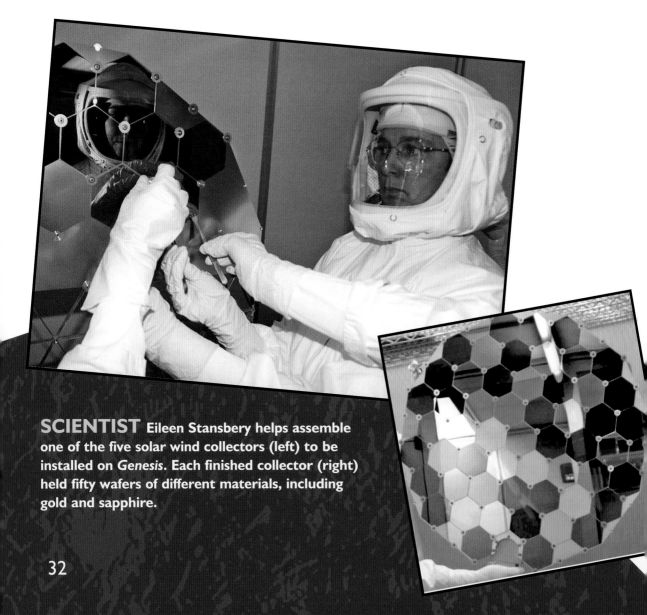

SCIENTIST Eileen Stansbery helps assemble one of the five solar wind collectors (left) to be installed on *Genesis*. Each finished collector (right) held fifty wafers of different materials, including gold and sapphire.

FAR-OUT FACT

SINGING ITS AGE

Did you know the Sun sings? Pressure and temperature changes inside the Sun make it vibrate, like a ringing bell. Sound cannot travel through airless space. But scientists can record the Sun's vibrations with scientific instruments. Speeded up solar vibrations sound kind of like humming. As the Sun ages, its voice gets higher. Studying the Sun's vibrations has helped scientists figure out Sol's age— 4.6 billion years.

Sun for more than three years. Even so, all its solar wind particles together only have the mass of a few grains of salt. After 884 days of sunbathing, *Genesis* closed its collectors and flew back to Earth. Once in orbit, the spacecraft released its precious capsule of collected solar samples toward Utah.

A SMASHING SUCCESS

The September sky in 2004 was clear above the Utah desert. Scientists and engineers gazed up, waiting for the *Genesis* capsule to appear in the sky. "We were anxious," remembered Stansbery. "I'd been working on this mission for a decade." A helicopter circled overhead, also waiting. The plan was for a stunt pilot to use a hook on his helicopter to snag the parachuting capsule. But the helicopter never got the chance. When the refrigerator-sized *Genesis* capsule appeared, it was tumbling out of the sky. "It's not supposed to tumble," said Stansbery. "We knew that something was wrong."

The capsule's parachute had not opened. There was no way for the helicopter to catch it. The space capsule slammed into the ground at 311 kilometers (193 miles) per hour. It split open, shattering the gold and sapphire wafers into thousands of pieces. *Genesis* scientists did not give up and go home. They quickly dug the capsule out of the desert dirt and flew it to a laboratory. Thankfully, the wafers had done their job. Most of the solar wind particles were safely buried inside gold and sapphire.

A failed parachute caused the *Genesis* capsule to crash into the Utah desert on September 8, 2004.

How did Stansbery feel when she realized the mission was not lost? "It still gives me chills down my spine," said Stansbery. "We did go out, collect a piece of the Sun, bring it back and we do have it here."

It took a lot of work and time to sort and clean all the broken pieces of collector wafers. But scientists are

SCIENTIST Eileen Stansbery examines the crashed *Genesis* capsule in the laboratory.

AFTER recovering the crashed *Genesis*, scientists carefully sorted and cleaned pieces of the broken collector wafers.

learning lots about what makes up the Sun. The *Genesis* samples are telling the story of the solar system's birth. One discovery is that the Sun's oxygen atoms do not match Earth's. The oxygen atoms in the solar wind are more like those found in ancient meteorites. No one knows why Earth's oxygen is an oddball. *Genesis* is revealing new mysteries for scientists to solve.

SUN-BLOCKING ECLIPSE

A total solar eclipse happens when the Moon is directly between us and our view of the Sun. The Moon casts a shadow on Earth, darkening the sky and covering all but an outer halo of the Sun. The Sun is four hundred times bigger than the Moon and four hundred times farther away, so one can block out the other in the sky. The shadowed area on Earth is very small, only about 270 kilometers (168 miles) wide. So even though there are solar eclipses nearly every year, they only happen over a small area. You will be lucky to experience one in your lifetime.

THIS photo was taken from space. It shows the Moon's shadow on Earth during a solar eclipse.

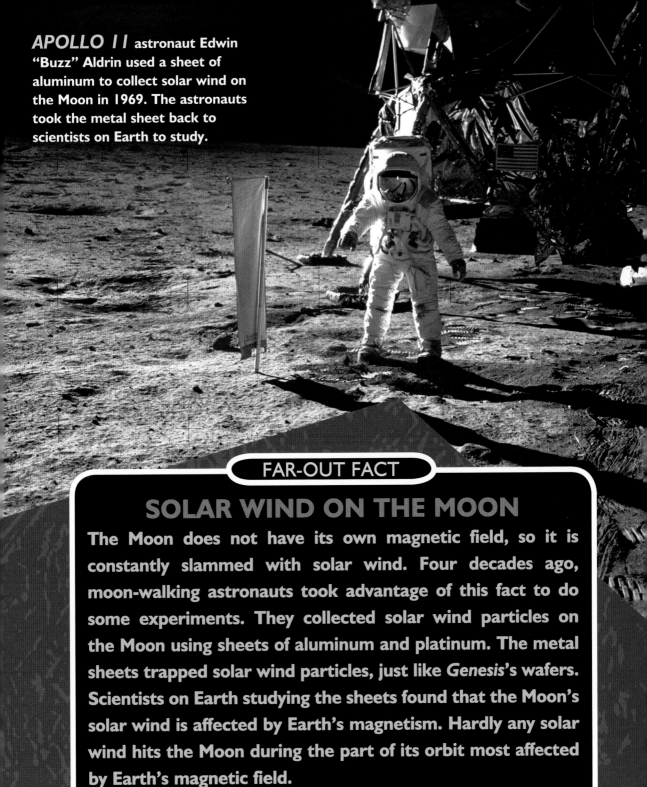

APOLLO 11 astronaut Edwin "Buzz" Aldrin used a sheet of aluminum to collect solar wind on the Moon in 1969. The astronauts took the metal sheet back to scientists on Earth to study.

FAR-OUT FACT

SOLAR WIND ON THE MOON

The Moon does not have its own magnetic field, so it is constantly slammed with solar wind. Four decades ago, moon-walking astronauts took advantage of this fact to do some experiments. They collected solar wind particles on the Moon using sheets of aluminum and platinum. The metal sheets trapped solar wind particles, just like *Genesis*'s wafers. Scientists on Earth studying the sheets found that the Moon's solar wind is affected by Earth's magnetism. Hardly any solar wind hits the Moon during the part of its orbit most affected by Earth's magnetic field.

CHAPTER 3

WHAT'S NEXT FOR THE SUN?

More than a dozen space probes and satellites are currently studying the Sun. In a few years, a spacecraft called *Solar Probe+* is scheduled to fly though the Sun's super-hot corona. "We are going to visit a living, breathing star for the first time," said Sun scientist Lika Guhathakurta. (See "Trip to the Sun" on page 43.) Spacecraft and solar telescopes here on Earth are mapping the Sun's magnetic field, taking 3-D images, tracking solar storms, and measuring solar wind.

Scientists are busy watching space weather and learning everything they can about the Sun. It is a very important star! Life on Earth would not exist without the energy created deep inside the star named Sol. The Sun bathes our planet in light as it spins between day and night. That sunlight heats our planet. Sunlight also fuels photosynthesis, which allows plants to grow. When you eat fruit or corn chips, you are eating the Sun's work! During photosynthesis plants give off the oxygen we breathe. You can also blame the weather on the Sun. Sunlight turns water into rain-making clouds, churns ocean waters, and creates wind. Our sun is a very special star.

FAR-OUT FACT

SUN-POWERED

Every hour, the Earth soaks up enough energy from the Sun to power the whole world for a year. Turning that energy into power that can light homes, heat buildings, run machines, and fuel cars is what solar energy is all about. People have used the Sun for thousands of years. Think about skylights, clotheslines, and drying foods in the Sun's light. Today, scientists and engineers are working hard to invent technologies that turn the Sun's energy into power. Unlike burning coal or oil, solar energy does not pollute the air. The Sun will likely power our future.

SOLAR panels like these make electricity from sunlight. The solar electricity can be used for lights, air conditioning, heat, or running computers or other machines. Some buildings have batteries that store the solar electricity during the day to use at night.

TRIP TO THE SUN

Solar Probe+ is a robotic spacecraft specially designed to withstand the Sun's heat and powerful rays. It is scheduled to launch in 2015. "*Solar Probe+* will actually enter the corona," said Lika Guhathakurta. "That's where the action is." *Solar Probe+* will likely experience some fierce solar storms up close. The spacecraft should still be looping around the Sun during the solar maximum of 2022. If it survives, *Solar Probe+* will give space weather forecasters some tips on predicting future storms and keeping astronauts and technology on Earth safe.

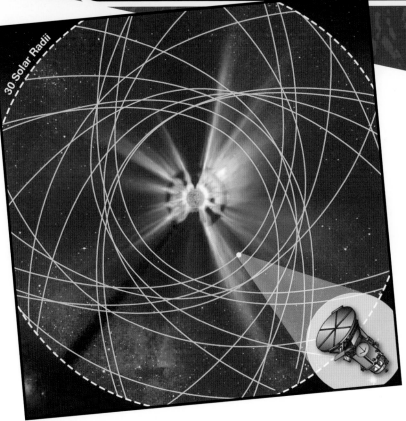

30 Solar Radii

THE yellow lines are the paths *Solar Probe+* will take around the Sun. Its closest pass, marked with a red dot, is about 7 million kilometers (4.3 million miles) from the Sun and within its corona. *Solar Probe+* will have a special heat shield to protect it from temperatures higher than 1,400 degrees Celsius (2,552 degrees Fahrenheit) and dangerous solar rays.

Words to Know

asteroid—A large rock that orbits the Sun.

atmosphere—The gases that surround a planet, a moon, or another object in space.

atom—The smallest part of a substance that has the properties of the substance.

aurora—Lights in the sky near a planet's magnetic poles caused by charged particles hitting its atmosphere.

comet—A large chunk of ice and rock that orbits the Sun.

coronal mass ejection (CME)—A massive cloud of charged particles ejected from the outer layer of the Sun.

day—The time it takes an object in space to complete one turn or spin.

diameter—A straight line through the center of a sphere or circle.

gravity—The force of attraction between any two things.

magnetic field—The area of magnetic influence around a magnet, an electric current, a planet, or a star.

mass—The amount of matter in something.

orbit—The circling path followed by a planet, a moon, or an object in space around another object; to move around an object in space.

photosynthesis—The process that plants and algae use to turn carbon dioxide, water, and sunlight into food and oxygen.

WORDS TO KNOW

★

planet—A large, sphere-shaped object in space that is alone (except for its moons) in its orbit around a sun.

prominence—A huge arc of gas erupting from the Sun's photosphere.

satellite—A robotic spacecraft that orbits Earth.

solar cycle—The eleven-year period when solar activity rises and falls, including solar storms.

solar flare—A sudden burst of light and energy from the Sun's photosphere.

solar maximum—The time during the during the solar cycle when the number of sunspots is highest.

solar minimum—The time during the solar cycle when the number of sunspots is lowest.

solar storm—Violent burst of activity on the Sun, including solar flares, prominences, and coronal mass ejections.

solar system—A sun and everything that orbits it.

solar wind—The constant stream of charged particles given off by the Sun.

space probe—A robotic spacecraft launched into space to collect information.

space telescope—A telescope that orbits Earth or travels in space.

star—A large ball-shaped object in space made of gases that shines by its own light.

sun—The star in the center of a solar system.

sunspot—Darker, cooler areas on the Sun's surface.

Find Out More and Get Updates

Books

Bourgeois, Paulette. *The Jumbo Book of Space.* Toronto: Kids Can Press, 2007.

Elkins-Tanton, Linda T. *The Sun, Mercury, and Venus.* New York: Facts on File, 2006.

Jefferis, David. *The Sun: Our Local Star.* New York: Crabtree Pulishing Co., 2008.

Mist, Rosalind. *Will the Sun Ever Burn Out?* Chicago: Heinemann Library, 2006.

Solway, Andrew. *Harnessing the Sun's Energy.* Chicago: Heinemann Library, 2008.

Solar System Web Sites

NASA. *Solar System Exploration.*
   http://solarsystem.nasa.gov/kids/nasakids.cfm

The Regents of the University of Michigan. *Windows to the Universe.*
   http://www.windows.ucar.edu/

Sun and Space Weather Web Sites

ESA and NASA. *Solar and Heliospheric Observatory.*
   http://sohowww.nascom.nasa.gov/classroom/for_students.html

NASA. *Living With a Star.*
   http://lws.gsfc.nasa.gov/

NOAA. *Watch Space Weather in Real Time.*
   http://www.swpc.noaa.gov/SWN/index.html

Space Science Institute. *Learn All About Space Weather.*
   http://www.spaceweathercenter.org/

Index